MW00436381

Infinite Black Suitcase

by EM Lewis

A SAMUEL FRENCH ACTING EDITION

SAMUEL FRENCH

FOUNDED 1830

NEW YORK HOLLYWOOD LONDON TORONTO

SAMUELFRENCH.COM

ISBN 978-0-573-69960-3   Printed in U.S.A.   #29934

MUSIC USE NOTE

IMPORTANT BILLING AND CREDIT REQUIREMENTS

INFINITE BLACK SUITCASE was first produced by Moving Arts in Los Angeles, CA from August 19 - 28, 2005. The workshop production was overseen by Artistic Director Paul Nicolai Stein, and directed by Michael David, Michael Shutt, Amy Thiel and Melissa Marie Thomas, with sets and lighting by Christopher Singleton, costumes by Ricky Lyle, dramaturgy by Michael David, and fight choreography by Ronnie Clark. The Production Stage Manager was Jackie Moses. The cast was as follows:

STAN KALINSKI . . . . Dale Duko

"KAL" KALINSKI . . . . Noah Schuffman

DONNA KALINSKI . . . . Christel Joy Johnson

DAN HANLON . . . . Brian Weir

STEPHEN MILLER . . . . Jeremy Gabriel

JANIE KALINSKI . . . . Christel Joy Johnson

JOE STRICKLIN . . . . Ronnie Clark

KATIE LIU . . . . Laura Buckles

TONY LIU . . . . Harry Du Young

LIZ MILLER . . . . Evie Hammer

FRANK HARPER . . . . Jon Amirkhan

FATHER SEBASTIAN . . . . Herman Poppe

APRIL MERRIWEATHER . . . . Molly Levine

JAKE HARRISON . . . . DG Bannon

ANNE HARRISON . . . . Mary Borrell

MARY OLIVER . . . . Daria Balling

INFINITE BLACK SUITCASE was subsequently produced by TheSpyAnts at the Lillian Theatre in Hollywood, CA on April 6, 2007. The performance was directed by Danny Parker-Lopes, with sets by David Fofi, lighting by Kimberly Negrete, costumes by Marina Mouhibian, and sound by Darcy Halsey. The Production Stage Managers were W. Shay Hammond and Madelynn Fattibene. The cast was as follows:

STAN KALINSKI . . . . Ken Arquelio

"KAL" KALINSKI . . . . Linc Hand

DONNA KALINSKI . . . . Darcy Halsey

DAN HANLON . . . . Eric Bunton

STEPHEN MILLER . . . . Jerry Pappas

JANIE KALINSKI . . . . Marina Mouhibian

JOE STRICKLIN . . . . Ryan Churchill

KATIE LIU . . . . Darcy Halsey

TONY LIU . . . . Kim Estes

LIZ MILLER . . . . Addi Gaash

FRANK HARPER . . . . Hal Perry

FATHER SEBASTIAN . . . . Bill J. Stevens

APRIL MERRIWEATHER . . . . Dawn Merkel

JAKE HARRISON . . . . Rich Williams

ANNE HARRISON . . . . Anita Khanzadian

MARY OLIVER . . . . Tammy Kaitz

AUTHOR'S NOTES

Infinite Black Suitcase takes place over the course of a single day in a single small town in Oregon, and we see events in the order they happen. Its characters can be grouped into the following five storylines:

STORYLINES:

Storyline 1: The Kalinskis
1. Porch Talk
3. Dress Black
7. Fragile
14. Geraniums

Storyline 2: Miller/Hanlon
2. And All the Roses Falling
6. Planting
9. Promises
13. Fourth Watch
14. Geraniums

Storyline 3: Liu/Stricklin
4. The Death of Ex
5. Gin
11. Six Bottles of Heineken After the Silverado
12. The Five Watches of the Night

Freestanding Scenes
8. The Last Four Things My Father Held Against Me
10. American Family

ORDER OF SCENES

CHARACTERS

STORYLINE 1

STAN KALINSKI (37) – An electrician. Polish Catholic. The dependable brother, who everybody leans on and calls first, ever since their parents died.

In scenes:

"Porch Talk"

"Dress Black"

"Fragile"

"KAL" KALINSKI (34) – Stan's brother. A truck driver with a local route.

In scenes:

"Porch Talk"

"Fragile"

"The Five Watches of the Night"

JANIE KALINSKI (34) – Stan's sister-in-law. A physical therapist and runner. Her husband has just died.

In scenes:

"Dress Black"

"Fragile"

"Geraniums"

*DONNA KALINSKI (35) – Stan's wife. Works at home and takes care of their kids. (*Voice only – can be double-cast.)

In scenes:

"Porch Talk"

STORYLINE 2

DAN HANLON (28) An English professor at the local community college. Quiet and bookish. He is dying.

In scenes:

"And All the Roses Falling"

"Gin"

"Promises"

"Fourth Watch"

"Geraniums"

STEPHEN MILLER (32) A landscaper. Hard-working and smart-assed, most of the time. He's been with Dan for seven years.

In scenes:

"And All the Roses Falling"

"Planting"

"The Five Watches of the Night"

"Fourth Watch"

"Geraniums"

LIZ MILLER (29) An interior designer. Dressed with casual quirkiness. Stephen's sister.

In scenes:

"Planting"

"Promises"

STORYLINE 3

JOE STRICKLIN (38) Katie's ex-husband. They have three daughters – 17, 14 and 12 – who are with Katie and Tony during the week and Joe on the weekends. Joe works at Wilco Farmer's Co-Op (which sells everything from chicken feed to John Deere tractors). He likes to drink a couple beers in the evening and fiddle with car engines with old Stones albums playing in the background.

In scenes:

"The Death of Ex"

"Six Bottles of Heineken After the Silverado"

"The Five Watches of the Night"

KATIE LIU (38) Tony's wife, Joe's ex-wife. Not Asian American, but took Tony's name when they married eight years ago. She is dying. She was a cheerleader when she and Joe were in high school together, high-energy and confident, not ditzy. She's paler and thinner, now, and has lost her hair (her head is covered in a bright scarf).

In scenes:

"The Death of Ex"

"Gin"

TONY LIU (52) Katie's husband, Asian American. He's a sales manager at the paper mill. Plays golf, and goes to competitions around the state regularly. Steady and even-tempered (except with Joe, who can light his fuse like nobody he's ever met). His marriage to Katie is his first marriage.

In scenes:

"The Death of Ex"

"The Five Watches of the Night"

MARY OLIVER (42) She was married to her husband, Roger, for thirteen years, but he died eighteen months ago. She hasn't been on a date since she dated him.

In scenes:

"Six Bottles of Heineken After the Silverado"

FREESTANDING SCENES

FRANK HARPER (45) He's worked at the hardware store in town for twenty years. A guy's guy, but personable. Today, he's been drinking.

In scenes:

"The Last Four Things My Father Held Against Me"

"The Five Watches of the Night"

FATHER SEBASTIAN (70) A Catholic priest. He takes his job seriously, but has a sense of humor. Fond of potlucks and college basketball.

In scenes:

"The Last Four Things My Father Held Against Me"

JAKE HARRISON (65) A retired electrician, who preferred working to retirement.

In scenes:

"American Family"

ANNE HARRISON (60) Jake's second wife. Elegant, even in unelegant surroundings.

In scenes:

"American Family"

APRIL MERRIWEATHER (24) Assistant Manager at Belle Passi Cemetery – an old pioneer cemetery out in the country where being assistant manager means you only have to mow lawn every other week. Young and sincere.

In scenes:

"American Family"

SETTING

A small town in rural Oregon.

The set should be simple, with various areas on the stage representing the various locations, giving the sense of a single world in which the whole play takes place. The stage should have multiple entrance and exit points, allowing the characters to pass each other as they come and go. Props should be bright and specific, representational enough that the items listed, by themselves, put us in the place where each scene takes place.

TIME

A single day. Now.

The action of the play should be continuous – one scene shifting directly into the next, with light and sound and props indicating the various locations where the play takes place.

For all of my beloved dead.

Scene 1: PORCH TALK

(Eight o'clock in the morning.)

(Kitchen of the Kalinski house.)

(When the lights rise, **STAN KALINSKI,** *wearing a bathrobe, open over dark trousers and a T-shirt, is sitting on the floor, polishing shoes – his own dress shoes, his wife's black leather pumps, and different sizes of little girls' black patent leather dress shoes. A shoe polishing kit in an old cigar box is on the floor beside him.)*

(Someone pounds on the kitchen door.)

*(***STAN** *looks up, then wipes his hands on a rag.)*

(More pounding. Insistent.)

*(***STAN** *stands up and opens the door to his brother,* **KAL,** *who's wearing jeans and work boots, an old Levi jacket and gloves.)*

*(***STAN** *looks at* **KAL** *for a moment.)*

*(***KAL** *takes his gloves off, runs his hands through his hair.)*

DONNA. *(calling out from offstage, in the house)* Who is it, Stan?

STAN. *(yelling back over his shoulder)* Kal.

DONNA. *(offstage)* Hi, Kal.

KAL. Hey, Donna.

DONNA. *(offstage)* You gonna come with me an' the girls? It's okay.

KAL. No. No, I just gotta talk to Stan.

DONNA. *(offstage)* He's gonna pick up Janie.

(beat)

Megan, what is on your face? What did I tell you?

STAN. *(to* **KAL***)* I gotta get ready.

KAL. Yeah.

   (clenches fist)

   There's somethin' not right.

STAN. *(wearily)* Fuckin' A, Kal, we've been over this.

KAL. There's somethin' not right! I saw him on Thursday.

   *(***STAN*** glances over his shoulder, into the house, then moves out onto the porch.)*

STAN. *(trying to keep his voice down)* You told me.

KAL. I'm fuckin' tellin' you! He came over. On Thursday, that was just...an' he helped me work on my bike.

STAN. An' you had three beers, an' he had two. I gotta get ready. She's been in the bathroom all morning.

KAL. Does that sound right to you? It was normal. It was totally normal. We had beers. We worked just like always.

STAN. Nothing is right.

KAL. That's what I'm saying.

STAN. That doesn't mean–

DONNA. *(offstage)* Stan, where are Chrissy's shoes? Her good shoes?

STAN. *(yelling back)* She wore 'em to school yesterday.

DONNA. *(offstage)* She's not supposed to wear her good shoes to school.

   (Offstage, **MEGAN** *throws her socks into the toilet.)*

   Megan! Why would you do that? Stan, will you please–

STAN. I gotta go. She's crazy this morning.

KAL. You don't give a shit. Your own brother–

STAN. I'm gonna hit you in the face.

KAL. Will you listen to me?

STAN. Just go, okay? Take a shower. We gotta be there at ten.

KAL. I'm not done.

STAN. We got things here, Kal. You gonna pick up Janie?

No. *(beat; turns to look in the box of shoes)* I gotta find Chrissy's shoes.

(KAL grabs hold of STAN's robe.)

(STAN's eyes narrow.)

STAN. What do you want?

KAL. I want–

STAN. *(overlapping; almost fiercely)* You know what I want?

(KAL looks down at his feet.)

STAN. I want to get through today. Would you just–

KAL. I want to know when you saw him.

(STAN turns away from KAL, but KAL keeps hold of STAN's robe. STAN turns back to KAL.)

STAN. I saw him...I saw him Thursday. Same as you. Okay?

KAL. Did he–

STAN. I don't know. Fuck. Jesus Christ, okay? He brought back my scroll saw. One he borrowed for doin' that new wall. That new wall he was gonna do.

KAL. The new wall.

STAN. Yeah. Months ago.

KAL. Yeah. Did he say–

STAN. He didn't say shit.

DONNA. *(offstage)* Stan?

(STAN looks back inside the house.)

STAN. I gotta go. Be at the church by ten.

(STAN swipes his sleeve under his nose, then puts his hand on KAL's chest and pushes him back a step. Then he steps inside the house and closes the door.)

(He picks up the box of shoes and exits.)

(KAL watches the door for a moment, then turns and exits.)

(Lights.)

Scene 2: AND ALL THE ROSES FALLING

(Eight thirty in the morning.)

(Bethany Community Hospital. Dan's hospital room.)

*(**DAN** sits in a hospital bed in a faded gown, propped up with pillows.)*

(He is pale. The inside of his arm and the inside of his wrist are bruised from IVs, although he doesn't currently have one in. He is holding a comb, but hasn't actually gotten up the energy to comb his hair yet.)

*(As the lights shift, **DAN** breathes out slowly, then reaches over and presses the call button that's clipped to his pillow. It leads to a red light, which begins to blink.)*

STEPHEN. *(offstage) (singing)* Oh, Danny boy – the pipes, the pipes are calling...

*(**DAN** looks up as **STEPHEN** enters, singing without regard to key, carrying a blooming geranium. He sets it on the nightstand.)*

STEPHEN. I don't think I've ever known the rest of that song. Don't you dare give this one away. It's a rare species of Eupatorium purpureum.

*(**STEPHEN** sits down on the edge of the bed beside **DAN**, notices the comb, takes the comb out of **DAN**'s hand, and combs **DAN**'s hair.)*

DAN. If you'd seen Mrs. Gelson's face when she came back from her barium enema, you'd have given her flowers, too. And you're lying.

*(**STEPHEN** pauses in his combing.)*

DAN. Even I recognize geraniums. Is she here yet?

STEPHEN. You said she said nine.

DAN. I look like hell.

STEPHEN. You said she was always exactly on time.

DAN. Like a machine.

STEPHEN. Then we've got–

  (*checks watch*)

  –twenty-six minutes before she gets here.

  (**STEPHEN** *leans over and kisses* **DAN**. **DAN** *kisses back, but then sighs and pushes* **STEPHEN** *away.*)

DAN. These gowns hide nothing. I'm not seeing my mother with a giant hard-on.

STEPHEN. (*pause*) You okay?

  (**DAN** *looks up at him.*)

  Relatively speaking, I mean.

DAN. I have to shit.

STEPHEN. You want me to get someone?

DAN. I buzzed half an hour ago, but Maria's the only one working today. Julie called in again.

STEPHEN. I could follow Maria up and down the hall, swearing in three languages, until she gives up and comes.

DAN. You don't know three languages.

STEPHEN. Swearing, I do.

DAN. You barely know this language.

STEPHEN. (*tentatively*) I could help you. I've watched how they do it.

  (**DAN** *looks away.*)

DAN. I wish she wasn't coming.

STEPHEN. She wants to come.

DAN. She thinks she ought to come.

STEPHEN. Giving a damn a little bit is better than giving no damn at all.

DAN. I don't actually know if I agree with that.

STEPHEN. What's the worst that could happen?

DAN. Don't ever say that.

  (**DAN** *knocks three times on the nightstand to appease the gods.*)

STEPHEN. She's your mother.

DAN. Not all mothers are like your mother.

> *(beat)*

I could shit this goddamn bed.

STEPHEN. She's your mother. She's seen it before.

DAN. Maybe you should...

STEPHEN. What?

> *(DAN lays back on his pillows again and turns his head away from STEPHEN. STEPHEN looks at him for a moment, then stands up and fiddles with the geranium, pulling off a dead leaf.)*

DAN. *(still turned away)* Did I ever tell you about my dog?

STEPHEN. Charlotte?

DAN. Before that. Strider. When we were in Port Townsend.

STEPHEN. He's not the one who chased the pig through Rodecap's fence...

DAN. That was Charlotte. Strider was my first dog.

STEPHEN. I named my first dog Spot, like any normal kid.

DAN. I should leave my books to the school library. You're never going to use them. Literary references go right past you.

STEPHEN. I do so use them. I put a large one under a begonia just this morning.

> *(DAN presses his hand to his gut and winces.)*

STEPHEN. Let me help you, goddamnit.

> *(STEPHEN reaches for DAN, but DAN pushes STEPHEN's hand away.)*

DAN. One day when I got home from school, Strider wasn't sitting on the front porch. He was always sitting on the front porch, you know? Three o'clock. Waiting for the bus to drop me off. He could tell time before I could.

> *(beat)*

But he wasn't there that day. I walked all over, down Brush Creek Road all the way up to the Adventist Church, calling his name.

STEPHEN. Danny.

DAN. A week later, something started to smell. Under the house. Indian summer that year. Port Townsend's usually not that hot in September.

STEPHEN. Why are you telling me this?

(**DAN** *looks down at his hands.*)

What, you want to go off someplace, under some house someplace, to die alone in the dark like your dog?

DAN. It would be easier than this.

STEPHEN. Fuck you! Fuck that, okay? When you were seven years old and your dog got run over, what did you want?

DAN. Strider just wanted to–

STEPHEN. You. What did you want? That little blond-headed kid, climbing off that big yellow bus?

(*no answer*)

STEPHEN. Don't you take one minute away from me, asshole. If that dog had been–

DAN. I hear you.

STEPHEN. –a bloody, broken, furry mess out in the fucking road, you still would've–

DAN. Stop it!

(*They steam silently for a moment, then* **DAN** *picks the comb up off the bedspread and throws it at* **STEPHEN.** **STEPHEN** *turns.*)

DAN. I don't want what you remember of me to be...

STEPHEN. All fucked up?

DAN. Yeah.

STEPHEN. Well...we don't always get what we want. I guess we've both just gotta suck it up.

(*Pause.* **STEPHEN** *rubs his hands over his face. He picks the comb up off* **DAN**'s *bed and combs his hair with it.*)

STEPHEN. (*quieter, now*) Look at me. Your mother's coming and I look like shit.

DAN. You're staying? To meet her, I mean.

STEPHEN. What's the worst that could happen?

DAN. I told you not to say that.

STEPHEN. *(beat)* Do I look like the kind of guy who brings flowers and splits?

DAN. *(beat; finding a smile)* You look fine.

STEPHEN. Do I?

DAN. Like Steve McQueen in one of those movies with fast cars in it.

STEPHEN. That's how you like 'em, isn't it? Smart-mouthed and butch.

DAN. All evidence to the contrary.

STEPHEN. Your mother's going to fucking adore me. She's not going to be able to help herself. I'm going to thump you if you give away that geranium.

DAN. I make no promises. Mrs. Gelson might need her colon checked again.

(pause; takes a deep breath)

All right.

STEPHEN. All right, what?

DAN. If you're staying, make yourself useful.

(pause)

Maria's never going to get here in time and I refuse to shit in front of my mother at this late date.

(STEPHEN lifts the blanket off DAN's legs and slides his legs off the bed, gently, so that DAN is sitting on the edge. He takes a white cloth belt off the nightstand and ties it around DAN's waist, knotting it in front.)

DAN. *(shakily)* How's the Schaeffer's yard coming?

(STEPHEN reaches his arms around DAN and grasps the belt. DAN holds onto STEPHEN's shoulders. STEPHEN lifts DAN to a standing position. They hold there for a moment while DAN gets his legs under him.)

STEPHEN. They have no taste. All they want is pink azaleas.

DAN. What would you put in?

STEPHEN. Bush rosemary, white tulips. Borders of creeping thyme for the bees to buzz and hum in.

(DAN *rests his head on* STEPHEN*'s shoulder. After a moment,* STEPHEN *rests his cheek against* DAN*'s hair.*)

DAN. That sounds nice. With the bees and all.

STEPHEN. The brilliant ones they never listen to.

(STEPHEN *backs carefully toward the bathroom [off stage].* DAN *moves with him. It is almost like dancing.*)

(STEPHEN *begins to hum* Danny Boy *again as they exit.*)

(*Lights.*)

Scene 3: DRESS BLACK

(Nine o'clock in the morning.)

(**JANIE KALINSKI**'s *house – her bedroom.*)

(There is a bed, with several black dresses laid across it. An open window, a dresser. There is a telephone on the dresser, and a picture of **JANIE** *and her husband, John.)*

(**JANIE** *sits in a rocking chair, wearing an old pair of sweats. She is drawn and pale and wears no make-up. She rocks back and forth with a rhythmic blankness.)*

(After a moment, someone knocks on the door of the house [off-stage]. Knock again. **JANIE** *does not react at all.)*

(After another moment, **JANIE**'s *brother-in-law,* **STAN**, *appears at the window. He is wearing a black suit and a white, pressed shirt, which isn't buttoned up all the way. A tie hangs loose around his neck.)*

(**STAN** *sees* **JANIE**, *and taps on the window.* **JANIE** *doesn't seem to hear.)*

(**STAN** *pushes the window open the rest of the way.)*

STAN. Janie?

(**JANIE** *continues to rock.)*

(**STAN** *frowns. Then he looks at the window frame. Then he climbs in the window. He squats down beside* **JANIE**.)

STAN. We gotta be over at the church at ten, Janie.

(When **JANIE** *doesn't react,* **STAN** *reaches over and takes her hand.)*

STAN. Jeez, you're freezing.

(rubs her hand in his)

You been up all night?

(beat)

STAN. Donna woulda stayed with you, but Chrissy's got a cold. They get sick, all they want is their Ma.

(beat)

You okay, Janie?

(STAN puts JANIE's hand back in her lap. She continues to rock.)

STAN. Dumb question.

(runs hands through hair; glances at clock)

We gotta get goin' if we're gonna get to the church.

(beat)

Donna's bringin' the kids. Marty an' Pepper are meetin' us there.

(JANIE doesn't react. STAN moves a little, to ease his knees, then sits on the edge of the bed.)

STAN. You want Pepper to come over an' help you get dressed?

(JANIE doesn't answer. STAN looks around and sees the phone, which is off the hook. He grabs it, presses the button a few times to get a dial tone, then dials. He listens to it ring...and ring...He hangs up.)

STAN. Okay, so maybe they left already. I woulda been here earlier, but I–

(STAN closes his eyes and takes a deep breath. He takes a handkerchief out of his pocket and swipes it across his nose, then stands. He looks at the clock. He looks at the dresses on the bed.)

STAN. Donna says she's sorry she didn't stay with you last night. She said for me to tell you. She said she's thinkin' about you. Everybody is. We got a hundred phone calls yesterday an' a dozen casseroles. Grand Central yesterday.

(STAN picks up a dark blue dress from the bed, then puts it back. He rifles through the clothes. He picks up a black dress, looks at it, then takes it off the hanger and shows it to JANIE.)

STAN. How 'bout this one? This okay?

(JANIE continues to rock.)

STAN. Janie.

>   *(beat)*
>
>   Janie!
>
>   (**JANIE** *continues to rock.*)

STAN. You gonna put this on or what?

>   *(No answer.)*

STAN. You gotta help me out here, okay?

>   *(pause)*
>
>   Shit.
>
>   (**STAN** *throws the dress on the bed and goes back to the phone. He dials another number.*)

STAN. It's me.

>   *(pause)*
>
>   Yeah, I know where I'm s'posed to be. She's not dressed.
>
>   *(pause)*
>
>   Yeah, we're still at the house! I'm tellin' you, she's not dressed. I get here an' she's–
>
>   *(pause)*
>
>   I know.
>
>   *(pause)*
>
>   Yeah, I know! But she's–
>
>   *(pause; sigh)*
>
>   All right. I'll figure somethin'. Kiss the kids, okay?
>
>   *(pause)*
>
>   Me too you.
>
>   (**STAN** *hangs up. He turns and looks at* **JANIE,** *then gets the black dress off the bed. He puts his hands on the arms of the rocking chair to still its movement.*)

STAN. So maybe you need some help today, right? When I busted my back that time, Johnny…

(**STAN** *pauses and looks down. Then he reaches in tentatively and pulls up on* **JANIE** *'s sweatshirt. He pulls it over her head.*)

STAN. We're gonna get you there, okay? I'm just gonna help you get dressed a little. I help the kids when Donna's late for work sometimes.

(**STAN** *unbuttons the dress, then slips it awkwardly over* **JANIE** *'s head. He threads her arms through the arm holes.*)

STAN. You okay?

(beat)

I don't know what the fuck to say. I don't know.

(beat)

Okay. It's okay. Lift up, hon, all right?

(**STAN** *eases the sweatpants off* **JANIE***.*)

(*He goes over to the dresser and opens up a drawer. It isn't* **JANIE**'*s drawer.*)

(*He puts his hand in the drawer for a moment, on his brother's clothes, then closes the drawer.*)

(*He opens a drawer on the other side of the dresser and takes out a pair of nylons, but throws them back after a moment. He finds a pair of black pumps under the dresser.*)

STAN. We don't gotta dress up anyway, right? Who's gives a fuck how we look? I don't know why I got this fuckin' suit on. Donna laid it out for me an' ironed up the shirt this morning.

(**STAN** *eases the black pumps onto* **JANIE** *'s feet, looks at her a moment, then takes a little black comb out of his pocket and combs her hair back from her face with it.*)

(*He looks at the clock.*)

(*He puts his hands under* **JANIE** *'s arms and lifts her to her feet. She sways a little, but stands.*)

STAN. Nobody's gonna start without us, right? So it's okay.

(beat)

It's okay.

*(STAN swipes at his nose with the back of his hand, then turns his back to **JANIE**. He takes out his handkerchief and rubs it over his face.)*

*(**JANIE** lifts her head a little. After a moment, she lifts her hand and puts it on **STAN**'s shoulder.)*

*(**STAN** turns toward her.)*

*(**JANIE**'s fingers walk, braille-like, to **STAN**'s throat. Slowly, she buttons his shirt, then begins to tie his tie for him.)*

(Lights.)

Scene 4: THE DEATH OF EX

(Ten thirty in the morning.)

(Bethany Community Hospital. **KATIE***'s hospital room.)*

*(***KATIE*** *has fallen asleep in her wheelchair.)*

*(***JOE*** *peeks into the room, then comes in. He looks at* **KATIE** *for a bit from over by the door, like he's trying to memorize her, then goes over to her. He reaches out toward the back of her chair.* **TONY** *enters behind him.)*

TONY. *(low, harsh voice)* Don't touch that!

*(***JOE*** *turns and glares at* **TONY***.)*

JOE. *(low voice)* I'm not hurting anything.

TONY. You're going to wake her up.

JOE. She wanted to talk.

TONY. She needs to rest.

JOE. She wouldn't have called me for nuthin', okay? She said she wanted to talk.

TONY. She hasn't been sleeping very well.

(They watch **KATIE** *sleep.* **TONY** *finally sits down in one of the chairs and, after a moment,* **JOE** *pulls the other a little bit away from* **TONY***'s and sits down too.)*

JOE. How did Amy's game go?

TONY. She said you were coming.

JOE. I couldn't get off! Jesus Christ.

TONY. Five to two.

JOE. They won?

TONY. Against.

JOE. They dumped off a load of feed at three thirty. I was bagging 'til seven.

*(***TONY*** *folds his arms over his chest. They sit there for a moment.)*

JOE. *(meaning* **KATIE***)* How is she?

*(***TONY*** *closes his eyes.* **KATIE** *opens hers.)*

KATIE. Peachy.

(*TONY and JOE both get up. TONY goes to KATIE, pushes back her hair, then kisses her on the lips. She smiles at him.*)

KATIE. Hey, Joe.

(*JOE goes to the other side of the bed. KATIE reaches for his hand, then tugs on it. He leans down and kisses her on the cheek.*)

JOE. How you doin' really, Katie?

TONY. How do you think?

KATIE. I was dreaming about going on a ferris wheel in the fog.

JOE. That sounds nice.

KATIE. I couldn't see where we were going. But I had a huge, fluffy, pink cone of cotton candy.

(*beat*)

What are you two arguing about now?

TONY. Nothing. Don't worry.

(*KATIE reaches over and takes TONY's hand – she is holding both of their hands, now.*)

KATIE. I am worried.

TONY. (*trying to be reassuring*) It's going to be–

KATIE. (*sharply*) No, it isn't.

(*TONY looks down at the floor.*)

JOE. You want me to wait outside, Katie?

KATIE. I want to talk about the girls.

(*TONY looks up abruptly.*)

KATIE. (*to TONY*) He's their father.

TONY. I've been–

KATIE. I know! And they love you to pieces, Tony, but we have to figure this out.

JOE. What are you talkin' about?

KATIE. The girls.

> *(pause)*

> Give me a glass of water.

> *(**JOE** starts to move, but **TONY** grabs the glass off the nightstand and exits into the bathroom.)*

> *(**KATIE** tugs on **JOE**'s hand again, and he squats down beside her. He butts his hand against her chair.)*

JOE. Bars everywhere in this place. Looks like you're in jail, or something.

KATIE. Better that than rolling out on my ass in front of God and everybody.

JOE. You got a nice ass. Always did.

KATIE. Shut up. Tony's going to belt you one if you don't quit being an asshole.

JOE. Me being an asshole!

KATIE. Work going all right?

JOE. It's all right.

KATIE. *(pause)* You know we have to talk about the girls.

JOE. You're gonna be–

KATIE. No, I'm not. I'm not, Joe. All right?

JOE. *(pause)* They're my girls.

> *(**TONY** hears that as he comes back in. He hands the cup of water to **KATIE**.)*

TONY. He wants to take them, doesn't he?

JOE. *(standing)* They're my girls!

TONY. Who's taken them to soccer practice for the last eight years?

JOE. I've been to every one of Amy's games this season except this one, and all of a sudden you're–

TONY. *(louder)* You don't have any idea what it's like to be a full-time father. You're weekends only, and it's not the same.

JOE. I've been here this whole time, not Siberia!

TONY. Who sits with Sarah every night and helps her with her algebra?

JOE. *(almost shouting)* You think you're the shit, don't ya?

TONY. I think I can provide–

JOE. Now we're back to the fuckin' money! Just because I don't ass-kiss my way up the food chain like some–

TONY. You can't even make your–

JOE. When's the last time I missed? Eight years and he's still got it right here.

(jabs at his temple)

What kind of–

TONY. You can't provide for them like I–

JOE. I'll take fourteen jobs before I let you have them, you yellow fucking bastard! You already took everything else.

(**JOE** *glances down at* **KATIE,** *then at the floor, then glares back up at* **TONY.***)*

(The two men stare at each other, still breathing hard from their shouting match.)

(After a moment, **TONY** *turns and goes to the window.)*

TONY. I talked to Kate Hall last week about it.

(pause)

Dave recommended her. She's a lawyer.

JOE. I could find a lawyer.

TONY. You don't have to.

JOE. What do you...What do you mean?

TONY. You have all the rights, Joe.

JOE. I...do...?

(**JOE** *stares at* **TONY***'s back for another moment, then turns to* **KATIE.***)*

JOE. Sorry about the yelling.

KATIE. It's easier to take your yelling with morphine.

(beat)

It makes a whooshing sound in my veins when I press the little button they gave me.

JOE. You wanna sleep some more?

KATIE. We're not finished.

JOE. What, you want us to fight about some more stuff?

KATIE. You're all right with this?

TONY. *(turning; bitterly)* Of course he's all right with this.

KATIE. I'm talking to Joe. *(to JOE)* You're going to take the girls full time?

JOE. I wish you weren't goin' anywhere, Katie.

KATIE. Wishes and horses, Joey. Is that what you want to do?

JOE. I don't know! Yeah. I don't know...

KATIE. Amy gets home at three.

JOE. Three.

KATIE. Someone should be there.

JOE. You know I don't get off 'til...Maybe...Melanie could–

TONY. She has cheerleading practice after school.

JOE. She looks just like her mom. I wanted to stuff her in the closet when I saw her in that little skirt and sweater they wear.

KATIE. What are we going to do about–

JOE. You tell me, Katie! Jesus Christ.

TONY. Don't talk to her that way!

JOE. *(to KATIE)* You got a plan, right? You always got a plan, so just spit it out.

KATIE. I want you to split custody.

TONY. What?

KATIE. Just like we have been.

JOE. With you gone?

KATIE. Yes.

JOE. Why should I?

KATIE. Because it's what's best for Melanie, Sarah, and Amy. And if you don't want that, you don't deserve to have them.

*(*JOE *clenches his fists, then turns and exits.)*

(**TONY** *follows Joe to the doorway and leans his hand against it.*)

KATIE. Tony?

(**TONY** *exits, without looking back.*)

(**KATIE** *unlocks the wheels of her chair.*)

(*Lights.*)

Scene 5: GIN

(Eleven thirty in the morning.)

*(Bethany Community Hospital. **DAN**'s hospital room.)*

*(**KATIE** wheels herself into **DAN**'s hospital room. She pulls a deck of cards out of a little hand-sewn pouch that's hooked to the arm of her chair.)*

*(**DAN** is lying flat on his back, staring at the ceiling.)*

KATIE. How did it go with your mother?

(Silence.)

KATIE. I envy car crash people.

DAN. No, you don't.

KATIE. No. I don't. But I kind of do. Fast terrible is better than slow terrible.

(beat)

Do you want to play gin?

DAN. I want to drink gin.

KATIE. *(beat)* Have you ever gotten an IV from Julie? She see-sawed in and out with the needle for twenty minutes last time she did me. My whole arm was purple.

(beat)

You want to sit up?

DAN. No. *(pause)* I heard yelling.

KATIE. I'm trying to fix things.

(pause)

I should send off to Romania and buy them both wives with my life insurance policy.

(pause)

Do you ever think of your...of your...with someone else?

*(**DAN** turns on his side, away from **KATIE**.)*

KATIE. Are you sure you don't want to play gin?

(No answer.)

KATIE. I can't imagine either one of them with anyone but me. Tony likes his socks and underwear folded like they do in the Navy. He was never in the Navy himself, he just likes things a certain way.

(pause)

I've written letters for the girls, but I keep ripping them up. In the last one I wrote how to pick out cantaloupe and the secret to parallel parking and how to fold socks like the Navy. And it wasn't what I wanted to say to them at all.

(KATIE *looks over at* DAN.)

(He doesn't move.)

(She throws a card at him.)

KATIE. *(frowns)* You're no help.

(pause; sharply)

I'm sick and I'm tired and all my hair has fallen out and it shouldn't be my job to take care of everybody.

(beat)

Goddamn it.

(pause; wistfully)

Car crash people.

(She turns her chair around and exits.)

(Lights.)

Scene 6: PLANTING

(Noon.)

(Belle Passi Cemetery.)

(Bright, crisp yellow sunlight and short shadows.)

(LIZ MILLER sits cross-legged on the grass, reading a battered paperback copy of Leaves of Grass. *She glances at her watch, then turns the page and reads some more.)*

(STEPHEN walks toward her. He stops beside her and scritches her hair, then puts his hands in his pockets and looks around at the place.)

(LIZ looks up at him and smiles. She puts the book in her bag.)

LIZ. I was beginning to wonder about you. How'd it go?

STEPHEN. You never appreciate your parents until you meet other people's parents.

LIZ. That bad?

STEPHEN. Oh, yeah.

LIZ. You okay?

STEPHEN. Yeah.

(pause)

Okay, no.

LIZ. How's Danny?

STEPHEN. They didn't announce that he's going to make a miraculous recovery, so I guess we've still gotta do this.

LIZ. Stephen...

STEPHEN. I could feel his ribs through the hospital gown.

(LIZ looks down at her hands.)

STEPHEN. He feels like shit. And I talked him into seeing his mother this morning, who really is like a machine, I can now report.

LIZ. We don't have to do this today.

STEPHEN. Sure we do.

(**STEPHEN** *takes a bottle of whiskey out of the inside pocket of his jacket, unscrews the top, and takes a swig, then offers it to* **LIZ.**)

(**LIZ** *wrinkles her nose, and doesn't reach for it.*)

STEPHEN. Dutch courage.

LIZ. *(gesturing vaguely)* Don't his parents want to help with the...

STEPHEN. She didn't even want to touch him. I don't think she's gonna care.

(**STEPHEN** *takes another drink, then goes over to the place under the tree where there aren't any grave markers.*)

LIZ. No wonder he's so weird.

STEPHEN. That's a shitty thing to say.

LIZ. What? Just because he's dying, suddenly I can't talk about him behind his back?

(**STEPHEN** *doesn't answer. He looks down at the dirt.*)

(**LIZ** *takes a brochure out of her bag and holds it up.*)

LIZ. *(gently)* Here's the brochure. You want to look at the brochure?

(**STEPHEN** *shakes his head, without looking back at her.*)

(**LIZ** *lays the brochure on the ground.*)

LIZ. I love him, too. You know that.

STEPHEN. Yeah. I'm just...

(pause)

...tired. I shouldn't have talked him into seeing his mother.

LIZ. How could you know?

STEPHEN. You mean, besides him telling me?

(**STEPHEN** *turns around slowly, seeing what the view is like in all directions. Then he lies down on the ground.*)

LIZ. (*frowning*) What are you doing?

STEPHEN. Checking out the view.

> (*pause*)
>
> I can't remember the last time we were here.
>
> (*pause; remembering*)
>
> Grandpa.

LIZ. Aunt Hazel for me. You were in Missouri.

> (*beat*)
>
> You shouldn't just lie there.

STEPHEN. I'd never been to a burial before. Funerals, but not–

LIZ. Dad tended to want to head straight to the reception.

STEPHEN. It's really quiet here.

> (*pause*)
>
> Where's Grandma and Grandpa?

LIZ. (*looking, then pointing*) Over there. I found them earlier.

> (*They are quiet for a moment.* LIZ *shades her eyes and looks out.*)

STEPHEN. How much is it?

LIZ. Right here, you mean?

STEPHEN. How much?

LIZ. Six hundred dollars.

STEPHEN. A hundred dollars a foot.

> (*pause*)
>
> Six hundred dollars for what?

LIZ. Just the place. Everything else is on top.

STEPHEN. Yeah.

> (**STEPHEN** *throws his arm over his eyes to block the sun.*)

LIZ. You can plant things here. The girl said you can plant things in this part. I thought maybe you'd... you'd like that.

STEPHEN. I don't want the flat kind of marker. I don't like the idea of being mowed over.

LIZ. Okay.

(They're quiet again. LIZ scootches closer to STEPHEN. She tugs on his pantleg.)

LIZ. You don't have to do this today if you don't want to.

STEPHEN. Yeah. Yeah, I do. I gotta do this now, because I'm getting really tired. And he's gonna...

(beat)

I'm really fucking tired. And after...

(beat)

I just want there not to be anything else I've gotta do, you know? After, I just want to...I want to be able to stop.

LIZ. You can't just stop.

(Silence. LIZ gets up on her knees.)

LIZ. You can't just *stop* stop.

STEPHEN. Why not?

LIZ. You're still going to be alive.

(Silence.)

LIZ. Stephen?

STEPHEN. You can't blame me for not being thrilled at the prospect.

LIZ. You shouldn't say that!

STEPHEN. I shouldn't have said that. I'm sorry.

LIZ. Did you mean it?

STEPHEN. No, I just said it for the hell of it.

LIZ. You're scaring me.

*(**STEPHEN** sits up. He brushes leaves out of his hair.)*

STEPHEN. I'm sorry.

LIZ. You're just tired, right?

STEPHEN. Yeah.

LIZ. I can... help you with things. That would help, right?

STEPHEN. We take care of our own.

LIZ. What?

    (**STEPHEN** *turns his head away.*)

LIZ. Since when am I left out with the fucking Indians when you circle the wagons, Stephen?

STEPHEN. "Since when am I left out with the fucking Native Americans" would be more politically corr–

LIZ. *(interrupting)* Listen to me! Will you fucking listen to me?

STEPHEN. I hear you! I'm doing the best I can, okay? I don't know what the fuck I'm doing, but I'm doing the best I can!

LIZ. And you have to do it alone why? That's all I'm saying.

STEPHEN. I don't know.

LIZ. You don't have to do it all alone. You're gay, for God's sake. Since when do you gotta be so macho?

STEPHEN. Since always.

LIZ. Fuck.

    (**LIZ** *stares at* **STEPHEN** *for a moment, then bites her lip, and picks the cemetery brochure up off the ground.*)

LIZ. Give me your wallet.

STEPHEN. No.

LIZ. Give it to me.

    (**STEPHEN** *pulls his wallet out of his pocket and hands it to* **LIZ.**)

    (**LIZ** *opens it, rifles through the cash, then looks at the cards.*)

LIZ. These are good, right?

STEPHEN. What are you doing?

LIZ. Helping you. Even if you are dumb as a stump. Is this all right?

STEPHEN. What?

LIZ. *(gesturing)* This. This. Is this all right?

> (**STEPHEN** *puts his hands out beside him. He picks up a handful of dirt, looks at it, then lets it spill through his fingers.*)

STEPHEN. I don't want the flat kind of marker.

LIZ. I got it.

STEPHEN. I don't like the idea of being mowed over.

LIZ. No flat markers.

STEPHEN. *(pause)* Don't use the MasterCard. I maxed it out two months ago.

LIZ. No MasterCard.

STEPHEN. Use the American Express.

LIZ. *(finding card)* This one?

STEPHEN. *(laughing a little)* Business expenses.

LIZ. This isn't gardening.

STEPHEN. Planting. It's planting.

> *(pause)*

Leave room on the marker for me, okay? But I don't want it here until...

> (**LIZ** *nods, turns toward the cemetery office, then turns around and comes back. She squats down and puts her arms around* **STEPHEN** *and holds onto him.*)

> *(Lights.)*

Scene 7: FRAGILE

(Two o'clock in the afternoon.)

(The front room of the Kalinski house, which they never use.)

(A small table, covered with a crocheted doily, holds a coffee pot, cups and saucers, and a matching sugar bowl and creamer. Several old-fashioned, straight-back chairs are set around.)

(STAN leans against the wall, holding a small, delicate cup and saucer carefully in his hands. He is still wearing his dark suit but the tie around his neck has been pulled loose, and the top button of his shirt is undone.)

(JANIE sits near him, staring at the floor.)

(KAL pushes into the room. He is wearing the same clothes as before. He looks around, looks at JANIE, then goes over by STAN.)

(STAN watches him approach.)

STAN. Where were you?

KAL. I came in.

STAN. We waited half an hour.

KAL. There's somethin' not right about–

STAN. *(glances at JANIE)* Keep your voice down!

KAL. I wanna talk to the police.

(STAN grabs KAL's arm and pulls him away from JANIE, almost losing his cup and saucer in the process.)

STAN. You say that in fronta her.

KAL. I got questions.

STAN. What?

(KAL stuffs his hands in his pockets. They're quiet for a moment.)

KAL. When did you see him?

STAN. Thursday night.

KAL. Thursday night?

STAN. I told you. He brought back my scroll saw. He wouldn't come in the house.

KAL. What did he say?

STAN. *(pause; slowly)* He wouldn't come in the house. We were havin' fish sticks, like it's fuckin' Lent, an' I said, "I wouldn't come in for that either."

(They are silent for a moment, not looking at each other.)

STAN. He kissed me.

KAL. What?

STAN. On the cheek. When he went, he just–

KAL. An' you didn't think–

STAN. No!

(Silence.)

KAL. You think it was money? With the job an' all?

STAN. I don't know, Kal. What do I look like?

(pause)

I remember the first one I went to. Uncle Val. You remember? No. You were too little. Me an'...They took me an' Johnny.

(pause)

He looked like a doll. Like they dipped him in plastic, then painted him over.

KAL. I'm not trying to bust your balls, I'm just tryin' to–

STAN. I know.

(Silence.)

Janie called me first.

*(**KAL** looks up sharply at **STAN**.)*

STAN. I went over there and...

(pause)

STAN. I went over. I s–

(*beat*)

I went over there. I'm the one who called the police. I never called that number before.

(*beat; glances over at* **JANIE**)

She's all a wreck. I don't even know what to do.

(*pause*)

I don't know why he didn't tell me he was...he was feelin' like...

(*pause*)

He coulda told me anything.

(*Silence.*)

KAL. You never said you...you saw.

STAN. Yeah.

(*Silence.*)

(*Behind the two men,* **JANIE** *pulls her legs up and wraps her arms around them, and rests her head on her knees.*)

KAL. Nobody told me that.

(**STAN***'s coffee cup begins to rattle against the saucer in his hands. He lays one hand over the top of the cup, then abruptly sets it away, on a table.*)

STAN. Yeah.

KAL. Nobody said shit about that.

STAN. Yeah.

KAL. (*pause*) So, it's– it's true. He really–

STAN. Yeah.

(*They are quiet for a long moment.*)

KAL. Fuck.

STAN. Yeah.

(**KAL***'s face crumples. He turns his head away.*)

STAN. Fucking asshole. Cocksucking son of a bitch.

> *(beat)*

> He coulda told me anything.

> *(beat)*

> He bled all over the fucking floor. You don't clean that shit. There's no way to clean that.

> *(JANIE covers her head with her arms.)*

KAL. Stop.

STAN. You wanna know.

KAL. Stan.

STAN. He used Pop's gun.

KAL. No.

STAN. You gotta fucking know. You gotta know everything. He blew his fucking brains out. All right? Is that what you want to know? I picked him up in my hands.

> *(KAL shoves STAN.)*

STAN. It's right here in my head. I can't get it outta my fuckin' head, Kal, an' I'm trying to keep all of you– And you won't shut the fuck up for one fucking minute. You think you gotta know. You wanna know?

> *(KAL shoves STAN again.)*

KAL. Please.

> *(STAN turns and exits.)*

> *(JANIE rocks a little, in her chair.)*

> *(KAL wraps his arms around himself.)*

> *(Lights.)*

Scene 8: THE LAST FOUR THINGS MY FATHER HELD AGAINST ME

(Four o'clock in the afternoon.)

(The confessional at St. Mary's Church.)

(FATHER SEBASTIAN sits on one side of the black scrim that separates the two sides of the confessional.)

(FRANK, who has been drinking, sits on the other side.)

(They've already been talking awhile when the lights begin to shift. Well... FRANK has.)

FRANK. ...just driving. You know.

FATHER SEBASTIAN. *(getting a little bit frustrated)* Are you now, or have you ever been, a Catholic?

FRANK. I've been driving around all day.

FATHER SEBASTIAN. Because I have to tell you, that's usually who I get in here.

FRANK. Just around. Up Mill Street, over the hill. Through Bethany and Silverton. Ran out of gas out in front, here. Do people really call you Father?

FATHER SEBASTIAN. It's remarks like that, that tipped me off.

FRANK. You've never been an actual father-father.

FATHER SEBASTIAN. The Pope hopes.

FRANK. Am I keepin' you from something?

FATHER SEBASTIAN. Oregon State versus Michigan, but don't worry about it.

FRANK. Because I don't want to–

FATHER SEBASTIAN. Don't worry about it.

FRANK. *(pause)* So... this is where people...

FATHER SEBASTIAN. Confess their sins. Yes. Two to four every Saturday afternoon.

(FRANK takes a flask out of his jacket pocket, opens it, and takes a drink.)

FRANK. It's...hard to get started.

FATHER SEBASTIAN. We have a script.

FRANK. A script?

FATHER SEBASTIAN. To help people get started. "Forgive me, Father, for I have sinned. It has been however long since my last confession."

FRANK. Forgive me, Father. For I have...

FATHER SEBASTIAN. Sinned. That's the ticket.

FRANK. How exactly do you define a sin?

FATHER SEBASTIAN. *(amused)* That's why I like talking to heathens. I never have these conversations with Father Benedict. We sit there at the dinner table and fight over how we're going to get the Parish House re-roofed before it starts to rain in November.

FRANK. There are...things my father held against me.

FATHER SEBASTIAN. Sins?

FRANK. I don't know. We never went to Sunday School or anything.

FATHER SEBASTIAN. You missed lots of cookies, Kool-Aid and "Michael Row Your Boat Ashore."

FRANK. My father's a real bastard.

FATHER SEBASTIAN. Watch your mouth. You're in a church.

FRANK. He's a real...he's...not very nice.

(pause)

That doesn't seem to cut it.

FATHER SEBASTIAN. Family. Enough to make a man crazy.

FRANK. What do you know about it?

FATHER SEBASTIAN. You think I was raised by wolves?

FRANK. He just has this way of...He says stuff. Me an' my sister, Livie, we had to take his license away in October. I mean, he kept hitting his mailbox, he has this old Ford pick-up, and I couldn't keep his mailbox up. Every time I went over there, it was down on the ground, smashed up, God knows what else he hit driving around, an' I'd have to pound it out and put it back up again.

FATHER SEBASTIAN. He didn't like you taking his license away.

*(**FRANK** takes a swig of whiskey from his bottle.)*

FRANK. No.

FATHER SEBASTIAN. *(pause)* You said...there were things your father held against you. Maybe sins.

FRANK. I don't know.

FATHER SEBASTIAN. That's what you said.

FRANK. Maybe sins.

*(**FRANK** sighs, and puts his elbows on his knees and his head in his hands.)*

FATHER SEBASTIAN. Have you been drinking, Mister...

FRANK. Frank.

FATHER SEBASTIAN. Mr. Frank.

FRANK. No, no...just Frank.

FATHER SEBASTIAN. Have you been drinking and driving around, Frank?

FRANK. Why do you wanna know? Is it a sin?

FATHER SEBASTIAN. Falls under, "Thou shalt not kill anybody while driving under the influence of alcohol."

FRANK. I think you're fuckin' with me now.

FATHER SEBASTIAN. *(gently)* Why are you in my confessional, Frank?

FRANK. Maybe I'm sorry I was drinkin' and drivin'.

FATHER SEBASTIAN. You were talking about your father.

FRANK. I was. Talkin' about my father. Father.

(laughs a little)

You want a nip?

FATHER SEBASTIAN. More than anything, Frank. But I better not. Baptism at five.

FRANK. What's that supposed to do?

FATHER SEBASTIAN. Baptism?

FRANK. You people got an answer for everything.

FATHER SEBASTIAN. We've been working at it for a while. It cleanses you of your sins.

FRANK. Hey! Maybe that's what I need.

FATHER SEBASTIAN. I don't think the Millers would appreciate you horning in.

FRANK. Fuck 'em.

FATHER SEBASTIAN. Tell me about your father, Frank.

FRANK. He's Frank, too.

FATHER SEBASTIAN. Frank Senior?

FRANK. Big Frank.

(*pause*)

You ever...heard of this Alzheimers shit?

FATHER SEBASTIAN. Yes.

FRANK. Well, that didn't have shit to do with it!

FATHER SEBASTIAN. It didn't?

No! He was a asshole to begin with.

(*pause*)

FRANK. You hear me?

FATHER SEBASTIAN. He was a–

FRANK. Yeah! But later on, it...he started gettin' kind of crazy.

FATHER SEBASTIAN. Alzheimers.

FRANK. He thought people were stealin' his roses. He had roses out front. Well, they were my mom's, but...she's been gone a while.

FATHER SEBASTIAN. Who did he think was stealing them?

FRANK. Black people. It was weird, you know? We don't even really have any black people around here. And any thief in his right mind would go after stereos or tools, not roses.

FATHER SEBASTIAN. That's not something he held against you, then.

FRANK. You rushin' me?

FATHER SEBASTIAN. Miller baptism at five, remember?

FRANK. I don't gotta tell you shit.

FATHER SEBASTIAN. You wouldn't have come in here if you didn't want to tell somebody something.

FRANK. I can't tell my sister anything. Makes her cry, an' I hate it when she cries. Livie cried for two days after we took his license away. He called her every name in the book, you know?

FATHER SEBASTIAN. Frank.

FRANK. He's dead.

FATHER SEBASTIAN. Your...father?

FRANK. I went into his room this morning. To check on him. An' he was...

(pause)

...cold.

(FATHER SEBASTIAN crosses himself.)

FATHER SEBASTIAN. I'm sorry.

FRANK. He thought...last month, he thought I was stealing 'em. The roses. I mean, I don't know why he'd say that to me.

FATHER SEBASTIAN. He wasn't himself.

FRANK. No. No, but...

FATHER SEBASTIAN. He was sick.

FRANK. And he said I never should of divorced Margie. But he didn't know shit about it, you know?

FATHER SEBASTIAN. Did you call anyone, Frank? For your father?

FRANK. He never thought I did anything with my life. He thought I was a loser.

FATHER SEBASTIAN. You aren't a loser.

FRANK. *(angrily)* How do you know? Maybe I am! Maybe I stole his goddamn roses right out of the front yard.

FATHER SEBASTIAN. My brother and me put our mother in a nursing home two years ago.

(FRANK doesn't say anything.)

FATHER SEBASTIAN. We both have jobs. My brother has five kids. We couldn't take care of her. But when we were moving her – they had the ambulance come out to move her – she grabbed on to my collar and pulled me down by her. She said I should smother her with a pillow before I let them take her to one of those places.

FRANK. They reek, those places.

FATHER SEBASTIAN. It was the only thing we could do.

FRANK. Yeah.

FATHER SEBASTIAN. Sometimes there isn't a good choice. There's just a bunch of terrible choices, and you do the best you can.

FRANK. And if it isn't good enough?

FATHER SEBASTIAN. You did the best you could. You took away his license so he wouldn't kill anybody or himself. You checked on him when you could.

FRANK. You put your mother in one of those places.

FATHER SEBASTIAN. For three minutes, I thought about smothering her with a pillow. I thought about if it would be a better thing, but I couldn't do it.

FRANK. Because you're Catholic?

FATHER SEBASTIAN. Because she's my mother.

FRANK. Yeah.

FATHER SEBASTIAN. *(pause)* Come on.

FRANK. What?

FATHER SEBASTIAN. I'm taking you home.

FRANK. I don't wanna go home.

FATHER SEBASTIAN. I know.

FRANK. What about the Miller's baptism thing?

FATHER SEBASTIAN. Benedict can do the baptism.

FRANK. I'm...we're not Catholic. My father isn't...wasn't...

FATHER SEBASTIAN. I don't think I'll be defrocked for driving you home and helping you call the funeral parlor.

(**FRANK** *wipes his hands over his face.*)

FRANK. Is there something for the end? You said there was a script for this thing.

FATHER SEBASTIAN. *(pause)* We say "I absolve you of your sins. In the name of the Father, the Son, and the Holy Spirit. Go in peace."

FRANK. That's nice.

FATHER SEBASTIAN. We've been working at it for awhile. Come on, Frank. Let's go.

(**FATHER SEBASTIAN** *crosses himself as he stands and exits the confessional.*)

(**FRANK** *stands and, after a moment, steps out of the confessional as well.*)

(**FATHER SEBASTIAN** *puts a hand on his shoulder. They leave the church together.*)

(*Lights.*)

Scene 9: PROMISES

(Five o'clock in the evening.)

(Bethany Community Hospital. DAN's hospital room.)

(Bed and nightstand. Geranium in the window. IV stand in the corner. Portable oxygen tank beside the bed.)

(DAN sits in bed, propped up with pillows. He is pale. His eyes are closed.)

(He is holding an oxygen mask over his nose and mouth and breathing shallowly into it. [Note: ellipses in DAN's dialogue indicate he's taking a breath.])

(LIZ MILLER enters. She closes the door behind her, leans against it, then unzips her jacket and fishes out a little white sack full of donuts. She dangles it in the air for DAN to see.)

DAN. I don't think...

LIZ. I have glazed. I have sugar. I have chocolate.

DAN. I don't like chocolate.

(LIZ drags a chair over beside DAN's bed, sets the sack on the bed, and rips it open.)

LIZ. Twist?

DAN. What are you...doing here?

LIZ. I can't say hello? And bring donuts?

DAN. Not without...an ulterior motive.

LIZ. Fine way to think about your sister-in-law.

(pause)

I'm worried about Stephen.

DAN. About Stephen?

LIZ. I know what's wrong with you.

(LIZ opens up some napkins, spreads them out on the bed, then sets a sugar twist on them. She tears off a little piece and hands it to DAN.)

(DAN looks at it for a moment, then eats it. He closes his eyes, smiles, and sighs.)

LIZ. What's with the oxygen?

DAN. *(opening eyes suddenly)* He isn't sick.

LIZ. What? No! No. He's fine. I mean, it's not that.

DAN. I don't think I could–

LIZ. It's not that. It's...

(pause)

...hard to talk about.

DAN. You never have trouble... talking. Most of the time... you won't...

LIZ. He's sorry about the mom thing.

(DAN puts the oxygen back over his mouth.)

LIZ. Really. He thought–

DAN. My mother would...be like your mother.

LIZ. He didn't know.

DAN. I told him it's okay.

LIZ. Is it?

DAN. *(beat)* No. But I'm...not mad at him.

LIZ. You weren't on oxygen this morning. He would have said.

DAN. Just–

(pause)

–long day.

LIZ. Want me to go?

(DAN pushes the donut bag toward LIZ. She tears off another piece of twist and gives it to DAN, then picks out a chocolate donut for herself.)

DAN. Why do you think some...thing's wrong?

LIZ. I shouldn't talk to you about this. You're probably the last person I should talk about this to, and here I am, fucking it up. With donuts.

DAN. Spill.

LIZ. I totally don't know who else I'd talk to, though. Mom only wants to talk about nice things, like she can make everything else not exist if she refuses to talk about it.

DAN. Liz.

LIZ. He doesn't want to keep on... well... being alive after you die.

DAN. He...said that?

LIZ. Kind of. Yeah. He pretty much did.

*(They are quiet for a moment. **LIZ** breaks off another piece of donut and hands it to **DAN**.)*

*(**DAN** takes the piece of donut and looks at it, but doesn't eat it. He lays his hand on the sheet.)*

DAN. Once more... unto the breach, dear friends.

LIZ. What are you going to do?

DAN. I don't know!

LIZ. I'm worried! Okay?

DAN. Yes.

LIZ. I wasn't asking your permission.

DAN. Yes, I know... you're worried. I can... see, you're...

*(**DAN** starts to cough, then has trouble catching his breath. He puts the mask back over his face.)*

LIZ. I'm sorry. I know you're–

(beat)

I'm just–

DAN. Worried.

LIZ. He really likes you, you know. He finally found somebody he really likes, and then... It's not fair. He said–

(beat)

–he said he's really tired.

*(**LIZ** sniffs, then takes a big bite of donut. Chews it.)*

*(**DAN** lies back and breathes into his mask.)*

LIZ. If I keep being this fucking sad for the two of you, I'm going to weigh 300 pounds.

DAN. Go away, Lizzie. Okay?

(LIZ picks up the donut sack. Before she can stand, DAN grabs her hand and kisses it.)

LIZ. What are you going to do?

DAN. I don't know. I have to... think.

LIZ. But something.

DAN. Yes.

LIZ. Thank you.

DAN. Yes.

LIZ. Love you.

(DAN smiles at LIZ.)

(LIZ exits.)

(DAN sighs, and puts the mask over his face, and closes his eyes.)

(Lights.)

Scene 10: AMERICAN FAMILY

(Six o'clock in the evening.)

(Belle Passi Cemetery.)

(**APRIL MERRIWEATHER** *stands awkwardly near* **JAKE HARRISON**. *Waiting.*)

(And waiting.)

(She rifles through the brochures in her clipboard, then waits some more.)

APRIL. *(conversationally)* My first burial? Didn't go very well. I mean the first one I did myself. And it was really bad, because I'd lost fourteen other jobs before I got this one. I'm just not a secretary kind of person. Or a cashier. Really, anything with machines is not good. And I really liked it here. Everybody was so nice! I mean, some of them were sad, because their people had just died, but nice! And it's outside. And there are flowers all the time. That day, Mrs. Koger – she's my boss – Mrs. Koger had to go pick up a deceased person over at Crendall's. And Ralph doesn't talk, really, he mows the lawns, so he couldn't do the burial, because you have to talk to the people. And I couldn't pick up the deceased person, because I don't drive. Well, I used to drive, but... Really, anything with machines is not good.

(**JAKE** *takes a step away from* **APRIL** *when she pauses, but she follows. He stops.*)

I'd seen Mrs. Koger do burials, so I knew what to do.

(gestures with clipboard)

It's not hard. It didn't seem like it would be hard. I came in super-early and made sure Ralph had dug the hole. That's not something I would have thought to do ahead of time, but Mrs. Koger explained that sometimes you hit a tree root while you're digging and people get distressed if you bring out the chainsaw. It was just a burial of cremains, which you don't have to have a very big hole for. Cremains is short for cremated remains.

(beat)

Anyway, I had everything all ready. The weatherman had said it might rain, but it wasn't raining, just blowing a little. And the lady came. All alone. I don't know if she didn't have anybody or she didn't want anybody. I took her over there. It was in the new East Section, kind of up on a little rise. Then I got the ashes. I mean cremains. With ashes, some people want them in a container, but you can just put the ashes right in the ground, and that's what she asked for, so they come in this plastic bag.

(indicates size – heavier and larger than a gallon of milk)

Mrs. Koger said to just watch, and usually they give you a sign when they're ready. When the lady looked up at me, I knew it was time – so I unfastened the top of the bag, and started tipping it out into the hole – and half of her father blew away! Just – blew away!

(puts hand to mouth)

I felt so bad. I didn't even think about losing my job, I just held onto the bag really tight so I wouldn't lose any more of him.

(beat)

And then I saw that the lady was laughing. "It's all right, dear," she said. "He was a bit of a blow-hard."

(pause)

I've been working here two years now. Longer than anyplace, ever. It's nice. There's always flowers.

*(**ANNE** approaches, walking carefully across the grass.)*

APRIL. Oh! There she is.

(JAKE moves away from APRIL [relieved] and goes to ANNE.)

(He helps her over to the place where he's been standing. She keeps hold of his arm.)

JAKE. You all right?

ANNE. Don't fuss.

(JAKE frowns at ANNE, then points over her shoulder.)

JAKE. Birds nesting in that holly tree.

ANNE. What kind?

JAKE. Robins. See the tinsel?

ANNE. We haven't been here since November.

(APRIL steps forward.)

APRIL. Mr. and Mrs. Harrison, I'm sorry this is so complicated. I didn't realize, when we talked on the phone...

ANNE. *(gently)* You're sure you couldn't squeeze us in, dear?

APRIL. There are very strict rules. The size of the space means that only two... well, caskets... are allowed.

JAKE. How about if I slip you a twenty under the table?

APRIL. Mr. Harrison, there are very strict rules. We could lose our license.

ANNE. I really don't know what we're going to do.

APRIL. You don't have to decide today. If you'd like to think about it, I mean.

(ANNE and JAKE glance at each other.)

ANNE. We'll do it today.

JAKE. All the places beside us are taken?

ANNE. That's a good thought. Like double parking.

APRIL. They are taken. This is an older part of the cemetery... we've opened up four new fields since this one.

JAKE. Jeannie died in '74.

(ANNE presses closer to JAKE.)

I remember picking this spot out. Ross drove me. It was raining.

ANNE. What else can we do, April?

APRIL. Well...there's cremation. Some people scatter the ashes, but you can bury them if you'd like to. And...

(beat)

Well...they don't take so much room.

ANNE. The Church says it isn't wrong anymore, but I distinctly remember Sister Mary Alice telling us, in Catechism, that on the Day, you had to have a body for your spirit to come back to.

JAKE. You don't have to do it. She said there's room for two caskets.

ANNE. You mean, you'd do it?

JAKE. I could do it.

ANNE. (shakes her head) That wouldn't be decent.

JAKE. What do you mean, decent?

ANNE. Decent. It wouldn't be decent. Jeannie and me lying there together?

JAKE. I don't think you'd be getting up to anything.

ANNE. It isn't decent. I'm *your* wife.

APRIL. There isn't room on the headstone, either. I mean, there's room for one other name, but not two. But the stone can be changed.

JAKE. Complicated.

ANNE. I thought we'd just come in and sign some papers.

JAKE. Sign a check.

APRIL. (checking watch) Mr. and Mrs. Harrison? I need to talk with Ralph a minute. He was going to start the water at six fifteen, and I don't want you to get watered. Will you excuse me?

ANNE. Go on.

(APRIL exits.)

(JAKE and ANNE stand there for a moment.)

ANNE. I need to sit down, Jake.

(JAKE takes off his jacket and lays it on a bench, then helps ANNE to sit. He sits down beside her and puts his hand on hers.)

JAKE. You all right?

ANNE. I just needed to sit down.

(JAKE looks up toward the holly tree with the bird in it again, and, seeing him looking, ANNE looks, too.)

ANNE. Prickly place to build a nest.

JAKE. I was thirty-six years old when she died.

ANNE. I remember.

(pause)

I brought you a casserole.

JAKE. Did you?

ANNE. She and I were on the PTA together for a year or two. I liked Jeannie. I didn't know her very well, but I liked her.

JAKE. *(teasing)* Don't want to lay with her, though.

ANNE. I'm old-fashioned that way. You knew I was old-fashioned when you married me.

JAKE. I guess I did.

(They are quiet for a little while.)

ANNE. I...talked with Ross this morning. While you were down mowing the church yard.

(pause)

He wants you to have a beer with him tonight.

JAKE. He does, does he?

ANNE. Yes.

(JAKE is silent. He takes a deep breath.)

ANNE. Are you all right?

JAKE. I don't think I am.

(ANNE puts her left hand to her face. She turns her head away from JAKE.)

(**JAKE** *turns toward her.*)

JAKE. Don't cry. I'm–

ANNE. Give me your handkerchief.

JAKE. Anne...

(**ANNE** *puts her right hand to her face and reaches out her left. It is bloody.*)

(**JAKE** *puts his hand in his pocket immediately and puts his handkerchief in* **ANNE**'s *hand. She presses it to her nose.*)

JAKE. Anne!

ANNE. It's just a nosebleed.

JAKE. *(taking* **ANN**'s *arm)* Let's go.

ANNE. Go where?

JAKE. To the hospital. We need to–

ANNE. Sit down.

JAKE. But–

ANNE. It's just a nosebleed.

(beat)

We're going to decide this today, about this place today. We're going to get everything sorted out and taken care of today. So just sit down and start thinking about the business at hand, Jake Harrison.

(**JAKE** *is silent for a moment, then rests his hands on his legs.*)

ANNE. Do you want me to get my own?

JAKE. No! No.

ANNE. You still love Jeannie.

JAKE. Of course I love her, she's my wife. But that doesn't mean–

ANNE. I'm your wife.

JAKE. I didn't divorce her. She just–

ANNE. Died.

JAKE. Let's do this tomorrow. You're bleeding.

ANNE. I'm not leaving until I know where I'm going to be staying for the next two hundred years.

JAKE. *(beat)* Is that when God's coming down? Father Sebastian give you a date?

ANNE. Very few things stay sacred more than two hundred years. They'll build a shopping mall here, I imagine. On our bones.

JAKE. Don't talk that way.

ANNE. *(bitterly)* Some things stay sacred, though, don't they?

JAKE. Do you want us to be buried somewhere else? The girl said they have a new area opening up over by those fir trees.

(ANNE *takes the handkerchief tentatively from her nose, then dabs at her face a little with it.*)

ANNE. I don't think I do, Jake. Because then, after I'm gone, you'd have a choice again. And I'm...just not sure you'd decide to be with me.

(pause)

I hadn't realized that. I knew you held a torch, but I... hadn't realized that.

JAKE. I love you.

ANNE. Maybe you do and maybe you don't.

(JAKE *turns to face* ANNE.)

JAKE. I married you. I love you! Whatever I feel about Jeannie, I-

ANNE. What does love ever mean to men? I don't understand it. Robert thought it meant building things for me. A tall, white house with a big red barn. A gazebo in the front yard with Martha Washington roses growing on it. I'd sit on the bench in that gazebo, all by myself, smelling those sweet roses, and listening to the relentless pounding of nails in the distance.

JAKE. I want to be buried with you.

ANNE. No, you don't.

JAKE. Can't I still love her a little, Anne?

(**ANNE** *winces and presses the handkerchief to her nose again.*)

(**JAKE** *picks* **ANNE**'s *purse up off the ground, opens it, and digs out a few rumpled tissues. He licks one of them, then begins to clean the blood off* **ANNE**'s *face with it.*)

ANNE. Things aren't very romantic nowadays, are they? Ex-husbands, dead wives, scattered children by various and sundry people who have usually moved to Florida or taken up tennis and don't have time for them. We live too long. That's what the problem is.

(**JAKE** *uses another tissue to clean the rest of the blood off* **ANNE**'s *face.*)

ANNE. I know this isn't easy for you.

JAKE. Men are supposed to die first. There's statistics.

ANNE. Do I look dreadful?

(**JAKE** *presses a kiss to her temple, takes the handkerchief from her, then stuffs the bloody tissues and handkerchief into his pocket.*)

ANNE. Tell me you love me again.

JAKE. You'll just argue with me.

(**ANNE** *brushes off her skirt, then examines the blood spots on her sweater.*)

(*She looks up suddenly, laughing a little.*)

ANNE. Strange bedfellows.

JAKE. What?

ANNE. I just thought of that phrase. Strange bedfellows.

(**JAKE** *stands, then helps* **ANNE** *up. He keeps his arms around her.*)

ANNE. Father Sebastian says there really isn't anything wrong with cremation. God can find you.

JAKE. I guess he could.

ANNE. It seems primitive.

JAKE. Vikings did it.

ANNE. Well, they were terribly primitive.

> (pause)

> Where's that girl?

> (JAKE *looks around, then pauses, shading his eyes.*)

JAKE. Coming across the grass like a steam engine.

> (pause)

> What are we going to tell her?

> (ANNE *looks at* JAKE.)

ANNE. That we're a modern American family. That's what we'll tell her. And we'll all go down together. Even if we do have to be burned up like heathens to do it.

JAKE. I love you, Anne. You're my wife, and I love you.

> (ANNE *kisses* JAKE.)

ANNE. Thank you for that.

> (beat)

> You will have that beer with Ross tonight, won't you?

JAKE. We're who's left, I guess. Me and Ross.

ANNE. Don't be morbid. Let's go sign the papers.

> (JAKE *looks at Jeannie's gravestone one more time.*)

> (*Then he takes* ANNE's *arm.*)

> (*They exit.*)

> (*Lights.*)

Scene 11: SIX BOTTLES OF HEINEKEN AFTER THE SILVERADO

(Nine o'clock in the evening.)

(The front room of **MARY***'s house.)*

(There is a couch at center stage, and a bookcase with a few photos and knick knacks on it to one side. One of the photos is of Roger, **MARY***'s husband, out on his boat, squinting into the camera.)*

*(***JOE*** follows* **MARY** *into her apartment. She is carrying a six-pack of Heineken in a brown paper bag.)*

(She puts her keys in her pocket.)

(He looks around.)

MARY. *(nervous, but trying to hide it)* Something to drink?

JOE. Sure.

*(***MARY** *looks at* **JOE** *a moment, then smiles a little and exits into the kitchen.)*

*(***JOE** *takes off his coat and lays it over the back of the couch. Then he walks around the place, looking at the books on the shelves and all the little knick knacks* **MARY** *has set around. He picks up the framed photograph of Roger and looks at it.)*

*(***MARY** *enters again, without her coat, carrying an open bottle of Heineken.)*

JOE. You said you hate beer.

MARY. But I'm rather fond of you.

*(***JOE** *grins. He holds out the photograph.)*

JOE. Who's this?

MARY. *(beat)* My husband.

*(***JOE** *drops the photograph, and the glass breaks.)*

MARY. Goddamnit.

*(***MARY** *kneels down on the floor, sets the beer bottle beside her, and begins to pick up the glass.)*

JOE. I... uh... didn't know you were married.

MARY. Was married.

JOE. You...?

MARY. I was married. I <u>was</u> married.

(She lays the pieces of glass carefully onto the picture frame.)

JOE. I'm sorry.

MARY. So am I.

JOE. *(pause)* I was married, too.

MARY. Have your beer. I'm going to set this in the other room.

(MARY exits. JOE sits, tentatively, on the couch. He looks back at the door.)

(MARY enters again, without the photograph.)

JOE. I thought it was... maybe your brother.

MARY. It's all right.

JOE. Should I go?

MARY. Drink your beer. I went all the way into a liquor store to get you beer. You know, I've never been in a liquor store before? Not even once.

JOE. You drink...

MARY. I go out sometimes and have a drink.

JOE. To the Silverado.

MARY. Give me a sip.

JOE. You only got one?

MARY. I just want a sip.

(He hands her his beer. She takes a large swallow. She doesn't hand it back.)

MARY. Roger drank Heineken.

(JOE looks at MARY a moment.)

(MARY looks at JOE's beer, in her hands.)

(JOE goes out to the kitchen and comes back with the six pack of beer and an opener, then sits down beside MARY. He opens one for himself and takes a drink.)

JOE. I visited a lot of liquor stores after Katie left me. This Arab guy had a place two blocks down. I don't know what it is, but lots of Arab guys have liquor stores and run cheap motels in this town.

MARY. You visit a lot of cheap motels in this town?

JOE. I go by. You can see in the lobby window that it's Arab guys in there.

MARY. Just checking.

JOE. I don't have a habit of picking up girls in bars.

MARY. I'm lots older than a girl.

JOE. You're pretty. I thought that when I first saw you.

MARY. Liar.

JOE. What kind of a thing is that to say?

MARY. People's eyes go up and to the right when they're lying. I read it in Reader's Digest. There was an article about the CIA.

JOE. You <u>are</u> pretty.

MARY. I recognized the green bottle. Heineken.

JOE. I usually buy Coronas. The Arab guy in my liquor store kept three little lime trees in pots by the window, and he'd give you a free lime with every six-pack of Corona. I'd usually just drink the beer and not mess with it, but free is free.

MARY. I was married thirteen years.

JOE. You know what I really thought when I first saw you?

MARY. That woman looks like she could use another drink?

JOE. I thought you looked lonely.

MARY. I really could use another drink.

(**JOE** *takes another beer out of the carton and opens it for* **MARY.**)

(**MARY** *toes off her heels and tucks her legs under her on the couch, then takes it from him.*)

MARY. You don't have to stay.

JOE. In high school, we always said we'd stay 'til the beer ran out.

MARY. I really did plan on sleeping with you tonight.

(**JOE** *balances his beer on his palm for a moment.*)

JOE. I've slept with a few people since Katie.

MARY. Did you...like it?

JOE. I'm a guy.

(pause)

It was different, though. We were married for eleven. She was a cheerleader. On the squad. They call it a squad. I never could play ball, bad eyes, but I came to every game after I saw her. She had this great little skirt.

MARY. You <u>are</u> a guy.

JOE. The first one after her, I just got really drunk and took home whoever would come home with me.

MARY. I'm getting there. Do you think we need more?

JOE. This is okay.

MARY. Is it?

JOE. Yeah.

MARY. It's not what you came home with me for.

JOE. Yeah, well. I'm not a boy anymore.

(pause)

Not that I don't want it...

MARY. I meant to sleep with you.

JOE. I figured. Bringing me back here and all.

MARY. It's a rotten thing to do. I should sleep with you.

JOE. You make it sound like doing laundry.

MARY. He died. Eighteen months ago.

JOE. *(pause)* Roger?

MARY. We were married thirteen years.

JOE. *(pause)* That's terrible. It's no picnic being left, but that's terrible.

MARY. It's no picnic.

JOE. I'm sorry. You want me to go?

MARY. I brought you home because you seemed kind. And age appropriate.

JOE. You thought I'd be okay to practice on.

MARY. That sounds awful.

    (pause)

    I guess I did, though.

JOE. Guys really don't get mad about that sort of thing. Weird women reasons. As long as we get slept with.

MARY. What if you don't get slept with?

JOE. We use our hands and lie the next day. It works out.

MARY. Was she pretty?

JOE. Katie?

MARY. That's a pretty name.

JOE. Yeah. She was the prettiest girl I ever saw. She wore this great little skirt. She's still pretty, actually.

MARY. You see her?

JOE. We switch the kids around between us on weekends.

MARY. You want another?

JOE. Yeah. Why not?

    (**MARY** *takes another beer out of the carton and opens it carefully, then hands it to* **JOE**.)

JOE. She got married again, boom, right after. Two years. That's not very long. She wasn't having an affair or anything, she just likes being married. Not to me, though.

MARY. It's nice being married. I didn't really appreciate it when I was.

JOE. Drink your beer, Mary-belle.

MARY. *(smiling a little)* Am I getting maudlin?

JOE. You're getting sad.

MARY. That's what maudlin means. Self-indulgently sad.

JOE. I say, fuck them for leaving us.

MARY. Do you?

JOE. Yeah.

MARY. Does it help?

JOE. You should try it.

MARY. *(loudly)* Fuck you for leaving us!

JOE. That's the spirit!

MARY. I don't think it helps.

JOE. It helps while you're actually saying it.

(**MARY** *sets down her beer.*)

(**JOE** *sets his down, too, then reaches over and takes* **MARY**'s *hand. She looks over at him warily.*)

JOE. Can I kiss you?

MARY. I thought I was as romantic as doing laundry.

JOE. Guys don't need romantic. I still think you're pretty.

MARY. You still think I'm lonely.

JOE. Who's it hurt if I kiss you? They don't care anymore. It's terrible, but they don't care.

(**MARY** *slides her feet down onto the ground. She pulls her hand away from* **JOE** *and shoves her hair back with it.*)

MARY. We're almost out of beer.

JOE. I've learned something since Katie left me. You want to know what it is?

MARY. I should have gotten two six-packs of Heineken. Is that German? Heineken?

JOE. You want me to go?

MARY. I don't think I should have gone into that liquor store. Now I know where it is. With the Silverado, I'd only ever stay for a little while, because I thought it would look pathetic if I sat there for a long time by myself. So I'd go in, I'd have one glass of wine, and I'd go home.

JOE. I better go.

(**JOE** *gets up off the couch.*)

MARY. *(loudly)* Fuck you for leaving us!

JOE. That's the spirit, Mary-belle.

MARY. Where are you going?

JOE. Home, to use my hand.

MARY. That sounds very lonely.

JOE. Story of my life.

MARY. That sounds very maudlin.

JOE. 'Night, Mary. Thanks for the beer.

MARY. Don't go.

JOE. Thirteen years is a long time. And eighteen months isn't very long.

MARY. Kiss me anyway. I'm very... lonely.

(*JOE looks down at* **MARY**.)

(**MARY** *turns away from him, and presses her palms into her eyes.* **JOE** *reaches down and strokes her hair with his hand.*)

JOE. Tell you what.

MARY. (*looking up at him*) What?

JOE. Next Thursday, I'll buy you your glass of wine at the Silverado.

MARY. (*pause*) All right.

JOE. Thank you for the beer.

MARY. I'm sorry.

JOE. It's okay.

(*JOE goes to the door. Opens it.*)

MARY. Joe!

JOE. Yeah?

MARY. You said you learned something since Katie left you.

JOE. Did I?

MARY. You said you did.

JOE. Maybe I'll remember for Thursday.

MARY. Next Thursday.

JOE. Yeah. At the Silverado.

(*beat*)

Stay out of the liquor stores, now.

MARY. (*smiling a little*) I will.

(*pause*)

'Night, Joe.

JOE. Good night.

(*JOE lets himself out of the apartment.*)

(**MARY** *watches him leave, then smiles, then exits.*)

(*Lights.*)

Scene 12: THE FIVE WATCHES OF THE NIGHT

(Eleven o'clock at night.)

(The Silverado.)

(The Silverado is a bar on the edge of town that usually doesn't get rough until eleven or so. They serve four beers on tap, six in the bottle, and wine for the ladies [what there are of them]. Scruffy wooden tables and chairs, and a jukebox in the corner [off-stage]. Country western music plays low in the background.)

*(**TONY LIU** sits at a table, arranging butter knives like bridges between the mouths of his five empty beer bottles with the intense concentration of the very drunk. He sips occasionally from a sixth bottle. His pressed white shirt is untucked and unbuttoned at the throat, and his tie hangs loosely around his neck.)*

*(**STEPHEN MILLER** drinks whiskey, neat, at the bar. Between sips, he cuts an apple up into smaller and smaller and smaller pieces with a silver pocket knife.)*

*(**FRANK HARPER** is leaning against the bar, already regaling Stephen as the lights come up.)*

FRANK. I'm gonna have to clean out my father's place. Gonna take months to get all the junk outta there. You never seen so much crap in a place, every single room. There's drawers you need a crow bar to open. Papers an' pictures. Twelve boxes of those goddamned *Reader's Digest Condensed Books* I swear nobody ever read. Clothes. Tools. Newspapers, and bills he never paid. Never even opened.

*(**KAL** comes in the door, rubbing his hands against the cold. Looks around. Sees **STEPHEN**. Goes to the bar and sits.)*

KAL. Hey, Miller.

STEPHEN. Kalinski.

FRANK. *(still to* **STEPHEN,** *but now to* **KAL** *as well)* It's dirty, too. The Alzheimers was getting him. I don't know. I guess that's what it was. Me an' my sister tried to clean up sometimes, but he'd get pissed off and start cussin' an' follow us around 'til we got pissed off and left. I found turds in the back of the garage a couple weeks ago. The people kind.

(beat)

Better me than Livie, though. She starts cryin' when she comes in the door. No sobbin' or anything, just... tears, leakin' down her cheeks.

KAL. *(to* **STEPHEN***)* Does he ever shut up?

STEPHEN. No.

KAL. *(to* **FRANK***)* Dude. Shut up.

FRANK. *(beat; to* **KAL***)* I've had a shitty day.

*(***STEPHEN** *begins to laugh. Then drives his pocket knife into the bar.)*

(A moment.)

STEPHEN. How about you, Kalinski? You have a shitty day, too?

KAL. *(beat)* You don't got any idea. Actually.

(to **FRANK***)*

You gettin' another beer or what?

*(***FRANK** *grabs two beers and moves off. Orbiting, with nothing to orbit. He goes and sits down at* **TONY**'*s table.)*

*(***TONY** *takes the offered beer, but remains focused on his knives and bottles. He hums a little – barely audible.)*

KAL. *(to* **STEPHEN***)* You, uh... You seen my brother in here?

*(***STEPHEN** *glances up at* **KAL** *sharply.)*

KAL. *(looks away, then back)* Stan. My brother Stan.

STEPHEN. This look like the Lost and Found?

KAL. No.

(beat)

It just looks like the lost.

(**STEPHEN** *pulls some cash out of his pocket and sets it on the bar. He moves toward the door.*)

KAL. Forgot your knife.

(**STEPHEN** *goes back. Pulls his knife from the bar, closes it, and sticks it in his pocket. Then exits.*)

(**KAL** *picks up a piece of apple and eats it.*)

FRANK. *(to* **TONY***)* Maybe I should just... dump out kerosene and torch the place. Just... whump. Throw down a match and burn the whole fucking thing. Just stand there under the oak tree an' watch it go.

(pause)

'Cause pawing through your parents' lives... It isn't something I want to do, you know? It feels like... What does it feel like? It feels like... When we were little, me an' Livie always knew when our folks were doin' it, because that was the only time they shut their bedroom door at night. Once every two or three months – that door would close, an' we'd look at each other and know.

(beat)

An' this feels like opening up that door. Pawing through their privacy, an' they're not here anymore to follow us around the house, cussing, 'til we leave them alone.

(**FRANK** *looks over at* **TONY**, *who is humming softly to himself again.*)

FRANK. You hear me?

(Between sips of Budweiser, and at odds with the Eagles, who have begun to belt out Desperado *on the jukebox,* **TONY** *begins to sing whatever random snatches of* The Five Watches of the Night – *a Chinese folk song – that he can remember.*[*])

---

*Please see Music Use Note on Page 3.

TONY. ...wu su li jiang chuan ge...

(pause)

... jiang chuan ge...

*(**JOE STRICKLIN** enters the bar, looks around, and sees **TONY**. He watches him for a moment, as he takes off his jacket.)*

FRANK. *(to **TONY**)* What the fuck is that supposed to be?

JOE. You got a problem, Frank?

*(The two men size each other up for a moment, but then **FRANK** takes a drink, and the moment passes.)*

JOE. Yeah, I didn't think so.

*(**KAL** glances back at **FRANK**, **JOE** and **TONY**, then leaves some cash on the bar and exits.)*

FRANK. *(quieter; snidely)* Back already, Joe?

JOE. Yeah, yeah.

*(**FRANK** turns back to his own table.)*

*(**JOE** goes over to **TONY**'s table, grabs an empty chair, turns it around, and sits down on it, resting his arms on the back.)*

TONY. ...jiang chuan ge...

(beat)

I don't remember the next line.

JOE. *(sharply)* What are you doing?

TONY. *(placing another knife)* Building a bridge.

JOE. Building a bridge.

*(**JOE** looks at the ceiling.)*

*(He gets up and goes to the bar. Gets a bottle of Corona [with lime]. He sits down beside **TONY** again.)*

JOE. So I get home from–

(beat)

JOE. ...well, never mind where I got home from. I get home and the phone is ringing and Melanie tells me you gotta be dead up on Brush Creek Road around one o' those hairpin turns because you never came back after goin' to the hospital and she wants to know if she should call the county sheriff or an ambulance. I've been drivin' around for an hour an' a half, lookin' for you.

(*TONY, still holding a knife, pauses in his building and looks over at* JOE *for a long moment.*)

JOE. What the fuck are you doing?

TONY. They look like you.

JOE. What?

TONY. The girls. They look like you. All three of them. Just like you.

JOE. Well, they fuckin' better.

TONY. They do.

(*TONY goes back to trying to balance the knife between his beer bottles.*)

(*JOE grabs the knife out of his hand.*)

JOE. Hey!

(*TONY rests his elbows on the edge of the table and pushes the heels of his hands into his eyes.*)

(*After a moment,* JOE *sets the knife on the table. He takes a drink.*)

JOE. I never said anything to them about you bein'...

(*pause*)

I never said anything to them about you bein' a Jap.

TONY. (*from behind his hands*) That's good, Joe.

(*JOE nods.*)

TONY. Because I'm Chinese, and they would have laughed at you.

JOE. They wouldn't laugh. They'd chew me to pieces for talkin' crap about you.

(*JOE takes another drink.*)

JOE. Just like their mother, all three o' them.

(**TONY** *brings his hands down from his face, and finishes off his beer.*)

TONY. Will you drive me home, or should I call a taxi?

JOE. Wait a minute.

TONY. Is there a phone here?

(**TONY** *gets up.* **JOE** *gets up and moves between* **TONY** *and the door.*)

JOE. I said wait a minute!

FRANK. Kick his ass, Joe!

JOE. (*to* **FRANK**, *but looking at* **TONY**) I'm gonna kick your ass if you don't keep outta my fuckin' business, Frank! Drink your fuckin' Kool-Aid and shut the fuck up!

(*JOE and* **TONY** *stand there for a long moment. Finally,* **JOE** *clenches his fists and sits down again.*)

(**TONY** *sits back down, too, heavily.*)

JOE. I need another beer.

TONY. There's nothing to talk about, Joe.

JOE. The fuck there isn't.

(*They sit there for a bit.*)

(*JOE shoggles his beer bottle, but it's empty. He looks over at the bar, but doesn't get another.*)

(**TONY** *looks down at his hands, twists his wedding ring around on his finger, then looks out – not at* **JOE**.*)

JOE. I'm their Dad.

TONY. Yes.

JOE. I'm just sayin' that, because... well, I am.

TONY. I never said you weren't.

JOE. You said a lotta crap back there at the hospital.

TONY. Everything's going away!

(TONY turns his head away, takes a deep breath, then picks up one of the knives on the table and tries, again, to balance it across the empty bottles. He takes JOE's bottle, and adds it to the structure. The knife trembles a little, tapping against the glass. He sets it down.)

JOE. Katie's tough.

TONY. She's dying. She is dying.

JOE. *(beat)* Yeah.

TONY. She's dying.

JOE. What do you want me to say, Tony?

TONY. I don't know. Nancy – the secretary at the mill – kept talking to me today, and I couldn't understand a word she said. I was looking at her, watching her lips. She could have been speaking another language.

JOE. You oughtta take some days.

TONY. And do what?

JOE. I dunno! I dunno, I never done this before, okay?

(They are quiet.)

JOE. Tell me about the game.

(TONY looks over at JOE.)

JOE. The game! Amy's game.

TONY. *(pause)* The Kalinski girl scored one and Amy scored one.

JOE. Amy made one? What happened?

TONY. I told you–

JOE. I shoulda been there.

TONY. It's... all right.

(beat)

The girl who was defending her kept kicking her legs.

JOE. Did you tell the ref? Clear Lake is always pullin' that kind of shit.

TONY. Just into the second half, Amy got past her. She went the whole length of the field. Nobody could catch her. Then she kicked it past the goalie and in. Then she did three cartwheels and the coach yelled at her.

JOE. That's my girl.

TONY. *(beat)* Yes.

(Silence.)

JOE. The thing about Katie is, she always gets what she wants. You can fight her all you like, but that's just how it is.

(TONY rubs his hand over his mouth. He touches his ring again, like he's making sure it's still there.)

JOE. Her an' me, we started goin' at it the minute we started goin' out. Fightin' and fu–

(beat)

–fightin' all the time, like two cats over the same yard, ya know? I think... I guess she minded it more than me. One day she just decided that was it, she didn't want to fight any more. And that <u>was</u> it. There wasn't any talkin' her out of it.

TONY. She said you never tried to–

JOE. I was pissed! She changed the fuckin' locks on the door!

(pause)

We're not talkin' about that. We're talkin' about this thing with the kids, right?

(Silence.)

JOE. Right. But I gotta know up front, okay, if you're really gonna do this. I mean, right. I mean, no gettin' drunk on a Tuesday and makin' Melanie cry her eyes out.

(TONY looks up at JOE.)

TONY. I don't know what to do without her.

(After a moment, JOE nods and pats TONY's shoulder roughly.)

JOE. Yeah. Yeah, I know.

(pause)

C'mon. I'll take you home.

(The two men get up and exit, slowly.)

(**FRANK** *turns and looks at the empty room for a moment.*)

(Lights.)

Scene 13: FOURTH WATCH

(Midnight.)

(Bethany Community Hospital.)

*(**DAN**'s hospital room. Bed and nightstand. Geranium still in the window. IV stand in the corner. Portable oxygen tank beside the bed.)*

*(**DAN** sits, propped up in bed with pillows. He looks stronger than he did in the afternoon. His eyes are closed.)*

(He is holding an oxygen mask over his nose and mouth and breathing into it.)

*(**STEPHEN** appears in the doorway, breathing hard – he's been running.)*

*(**DAN** opens his eyes and looks at **STEPHEN**.)*

STEPHEN. You're scaring the shit out of me.

*(**DAN** takes the mask away from his face.)*

DAN. I said everything was okay. You didn't have to–

STEPHEN. I'm going to throw away the answering machine. And the telephone. Every time they–

DAN. I'm sorry. I just... needed to see you.

*(**STEPHEN** moves to the window. He pulls a dead leaf off the geranium.)*

DAN. Come here, will you?

*(**STEPHEN** sits on the edge of the bed, beside **DAN**. **DAN** puts his arms around **STEPHEN**, and **STEPHEN** rests his head on **DAN**'s shoulder.)*

DAN. You've been drinking.

STEPHEN. You're really okay?

*(**DAN** nods. **STEPHEN** sits up.)*

STEPHEN. Just a little. Beer. At the shit-kicker bar down the road.

DAN. Liz came to see me today.

STEPHEN. *(pause)* She... tell you what we did? I did?

DAN. She told me...

(pause)

What did you do?

STEPHEN. She didn't tell you?

DAN. The two of you frustrate the hell out of me sometimes.

STEPHEN. You'll... think it's weird. Or bad. I don't know.

(DAN takes hold of STEPHEN's shirt and gives him a gentle shake.)

STEPHEN. I bought a place for us. At Belle Passi.

DAN. Belle Passi. The... cemetery.

STEPHEN. I wasn't going to tell you.

(DAN takes a breath. Then he picks up the oxygen mask and breathes into it.)

STEPHEN. I'm sorry.

DAN. You always tell me things. It's just...

STEPHEN. I didn't mean to tell you.

DAN. ...kind of terrifying.

(pause)

Come in with me.

(STEPHEN rubs his hands over his face. He takes off his shoes and jacket.)

(DAN lifts up the covers.)

(STEPHEN slides in beside him, carefully.)

(DAN leans forward, so STEPHEN can put an arm around him, then lays back on STEPHEN's shoulder.)

STEPHEN. Doris is going to be mad if she finds me in here.

DAN. Doris is always mad.

(beat)

DAN. Indian women used to... throw themselves onto their husbands' funeral pyres. I don't know if it was because they were sad, or that they were losing their place in society or their protector... I can't remember.

STEPHEN. That's not what I said. That's what she told you?

DAN. She's worried about you.

(**STEPHEN** *turns his head away.*)

STEPHEN. That's not what I said.

DAN. What did you say?

STEPHEN. I'm tired.

(*pause*)

God, it's been a fucked up day. I'm sorry about your mother. I shouldn't have ever called her. She's evil.

DAN. I told you that. You should listen to me.

STEPHEN. I listen to you. Okay, sometimes. I didn't know she'd be evil. People exaggerate about their parents.

DAN. Liz wants me to save you.

(*Silence.*)

DAN. Liz thinks you need saving.

(*Silence.*)

(**DAN** *pulls away from* **STEPHEN**. *Looks at him a moment. Then hits him.*)

(**STEPHEN** *pulls his arm out from behind* **DAN**, *pulls up his knees, and wraps his arms around them.*)

DAN. I don't know what to say. I'm sorry I'm–

(*beat*)

–I didn't mean to leave you. I love you.

(**STEPHEN** *closes his eyes.*)

DAN. Keep going, okay?

(*pause*)

I don't know how. I can't tell you how, I don't know. But I want you to. Stephen, I want you to.

STEPHEN. I'm tired.

DAN. I know.

> (STEPHEN *turns and lies down, so that his head is in* DAN*'s lap.*)
>
> (DAN *runs his hand through* STEPHEN*'s hair.*)
>
> (*Lights.*)

Scene 14: GERANIUMS

(Action is continuous.)

(As **STEPHEN** *rests in* **DAN***'s arms, the lights begin to dim on the hospital room, and come up, slowly, on* **JANIE KALINSKI***.)*

(It is day again. Some day. She is kneeling on the ground at Belle Passi Cemetery.)

(She has a flat of plants beside her – geraniums and marigolds – and a trowel, and some marigold seeds, and she organizes them as she sits there.)

JANIE. If you take anything from this whole experience, it should be geraniums.

*(***STEPHEN** *turns in* **DAN***'s arms and looks at* **JANIE***. He frowns.)*

(He climbs out of the hospital bed and takes a few steps toward **JANIE***.)*

STEPHEN. What?

JANIE. I said, you can plant things here.

(He looks at her blankly.)

(She gestures at the immediate vicinity.)

JANIE. That's what she told me. That girl.

*(***STEPHEN** *turns back toward the hospital bed, but it is empty, now.)*

(He looks at it for a moment.)

*(***STEPHEN** *sits abruptly. It is almost like falling.)*

*(***JANIE** *glances at him.)*

(She takes a small geranium from the flat beside her. She holds it out to **STEPHEN***, but he doesn't take it.)*

(She sets it on the ground in front of him then returns to her plants.)

*(***STEPHEN** *looks at the geranium.)*

(After a moment, he picks it up, and then he picks up the trowel, and begins to dig.)

(Planting.)

(Lights.)

END OF PLAY

OTHER TITLES AVAILABLE FROM SAMUEL FRENCH

SONG OF EXTINCTION

EM Lewis

Drama / 5m, 1f / Multiple Sets

**2009 Harold and Mimi Steinberg/ATCA New Play Award
— American Theater Critics Association
2008 Ted Schmitt Award for the world premiere of an Outstanding
New Play – Los Angeles Drama Critics Circle
2008 Production of the Year — The LA Weekly Awards
– Los Angeles, CA**

Max, a musically gifted high school student, is falling off the edge of the world — and his biology teacher is the only one who's noticed. A play about the science of life and loss, the relationships between fathers and sons, Cambodian fields, Bolivian rainforests and redemption. Max Forrestal is going to fail Biology if he doesn't complete a 20-page paper on extinction by 2pm on Tuesday — but his mother, Lily, is dying of cancer, and school is the last thing on his mind. His father, Ellery, a biologist obsessed with saving a rare Bolivian insect, is incapable of dealing with his wife's impending death, or his son's distress. Max's biology teacher, Khim Phan, tries to figure out why Max is failing the class. Helping Max, however, pushes Khim into a magical journey of his own — from the Cambodian fields of his youth into the undiscovered country beyond.

"Critic's Choice…artfully balances its theme of mortality between the intimate and the macroscopic…explores inner psychological states with remarkable eloquence and clarity…"
– Phillip Brandeis, *Los Angeles Times.*

"The interplay of the three [views on extinction] in Lewis' smart and honest script is one small push away from collective transcendence"
– Amy Nicholson, *LA Weekly*

OTHER TITLES AVAILABLE FROM SAMUEL FRENCH

THE HAPPY ONES

Julie Marie Myatt

Dramatic Comedy / 3m, 1f

WINNER! 2009 Ted Schmitt Award for the world premiere of an Outstanding New Play – Los Angeles Drama Critics Circle

Orange County, California, 1975. For Walter Wells, it's the happiest place on earth. He has a beautiful wife. Two great kids. A house with a pool. Contentment. Until fate strikes a devastating blow, leaving Walter with no reason to put the pieces of his life back together. He resists attempts to help, especially the unexpected — and unwanted — offer from a Vietnamese refugee named Bao Ngo, who bears his own sadness. Then, across a cultural divide, Walter and Bao find a game to share, a song, a meal and then a way back in this uplifting — and surprisingly funny — new play by a rising star in American theatre.

"Wry and affecting…Myatt's characters are so engaging that it's easy to push them toward comedy, which tends to reassure rather than surprise us."
– Los Angeles Times

"…Understated power of this gentle yet gripping dramedy…The most impressive element of Myatt's new work is the dexterous way she elicits emotional resonance by giving the human frailties of the characters a weight equal to their innate compassion and goodness. Subtly depicting the overwhelmingly difficult process of mourning and letting go, Myatt leavens the tragedy without blunting its significance."
– Backstage

OTHER TITLES AVAILABLE FROM SAMUEL FRENCH

THE QUALITY OF LIFE

Jane Anderson

Dramatic Comedy / 2m, 2f

Winner! 2007 Ted Schmitt Award for the world premiere of an Outstanding New Play — Los Angeles Drama Critics Circle

Winner! 2008 Ovation Award for Best New Play

From award-winning writer Jane Anderson (*The Baby Dance, Looking for Normal*) comes this "magnetic work of theater" (*The San Francisco Chronicle*) filled with compassion, honesty and humor.

Dinah and Bill, a devout, church-going couple from the Midwest are struggling to keep their lives intact after the loss of their daughter. Dinah is compelled to reconnect with her left-leaning cousins in Northern California who're going through their own trials. Jeannette and Neil have lost their home to a wildfire and Neil has cancer. However they seem to have accepted their situation with astounding good humor, living in a yurt on their burn site and celebrating life with hits of pot and glasses of good red wine. Bill and Dinah are both moved and perplexed by their cousins' remarkable equanimity. But their sympathy turns to rage when they find out that Jeannette is planning to take her own life to avoid a life of grief without her beloved Neil.

"Playwright Jane Anderson explores a myriad of ethical, religious, and moral beliefs, as well as (some would say) personal rights issues concerning life and death in her remarkable and completely engrossing new play, *The Quality of Life*."
– Terri Roberts, *TheaterMania*

OTHER TITLES AVAILABLE FROM SAMUEL FRENCH

ELEPHANT SIGHS

Ed Simpson

Comedy / 5m

Not long after moving to the small town of Randolphsburg, PA, uptight lawyer Joel Bixby is invited by Leo Applegate, an avuncular fast food connoisseur, to join a group of townsmen who meet in a ramshackle room at the edge of town. Leo has chosen Joel as a replacement for the late - and greatly beloved – Walter Deagon. Despite protesting that he's just not an organizational man, Joel finds himself mesmerized by Leo's ebullient manner and agrees to drop by - without ever asking just what exactly it is the group actually does. Determining that the meeting will at least help him network with potential clients, Joel arrives, hoping that the group's purpose will eventually become clear. Joel's confusion only increases as, one by one, he meets the group's surviving members who includes Dink, a perpetually gleeful little man who deeply loves his bald-headed wife and who is "in touch with his feminine side"; insurance man Perry, a former minister in the midst of a painful crisis of faith; and Nick, a volatile contractor who has recently lost his job and family and is desperately looking for some kind of miracle. As an increasingly anxious Joel is swept up in the strange lives of the guys, he struggles to figure out exactly why they've all come together. The more time he spends with them, the more apparent it becomes that each of them are just as lost as Joel. As the evening progresses, however, the regulars - and newcomer Joel - grapple with their own disappointments, offer comfort to each other, and, in the process, finally reveal the mysterious reason for their gathering. A group of delightful characters highlight this comedy about loss, loneliness, and the healing power of friendship.

"Critic's Choice...Don't let the surface banality fool you. The emotions of these men, however imperfectly communicated, are agonizing, their need for comfort and companionship as acute as hunger and thirst."
– F. Kathleen Foley, *Los Angeles Times*
SAMUELFRENCH.COM